Graphing Financial Information
How Accountants Can Use Graphs to Communicate

by

Anker V. Andersen, Ph.D.

A study carried out on behalf of the
National Association of Accountants
New York, New York

Published by

National Association of Accountants
919 Third Ave., New York, N.Y. 10022

Norma Frankel, Editor
Mandel & Wagreich, Inc., Cover

NAA Publication Number 82138
ISBN 0-86641-086-4

Foreword

During the last 10 years, more people have been turning to graphs as a good way to present information to managers and others. Managers overloaded with work and pressured to make quick decisions can save time by studying a pictorial report rather than by reading a written report. Plus, pictures or graphs sometimes can be more effective and have a greater impact on the viewer than can written information.

Graphs also help use one of the main scarce resources of management—time. The time needed to communicate and interpret the data is less with a visual presentation than with a textual or tabular report. Visual information can be comprehended faster, and trends and comparisons lend themselves to, and are more easily presented and understood by, a graphic presentation. Trends and comparisons are tools used to reduce the uncertainties in decision making.

This book is an updated and revised version of an earlier National Association of Accountants publication titled *Use of Graphs in Internal Reporting,* which was published in October 1961. This new book discusses which graphs are popular today and examines the use of computer graphics. It includes a review of current practices of graphics accounting information, and it lists individuals who provided information about current practice and the NAA chapters through which the contributions were submitted.

The report reflects the views of the researcher and not necessarily those of the Association or the Committee on Research.

Stephen Landekich
Research Director
National Association of Accountants

iii

Table of Contents

Graphing Financial Information
How Accountants Can Use Graphs to Communicate

Introduction

Graphs can present internal accounting data effectively. Because one of the main functions of the accountant is to communicate accounting information to users, accountants should use graphs, at least to the extent that they clarify the presentation of accounting data, present the data fairly, and enhance management's ability to make a more informed decision. It has been argued that the human brain can absorb and understand images more easily than words and numbers, and, therefore, graphs may be better communicative devices than written reports or tabular statements.

The primary uses of graphs are to determine trends and to make comparisons, either between actual and projected data or between different aspects of the activities of a firm. When accountants need to present these kinds of information, they should consider using graphs. Also, by their use of color and symbols, graphs can help to call attention to or emphasize some aspect of a report.

This publication is divided into two sections. The first is an introduction to graphic presentation and the second is a description of current practice. This approach is used to allow for greater selectivity, based on the reader's interests and background. The problem under investigation in this publication is how graphs can be used to improve the communication of management accounting information.

Chapter 1

Preparation of Graphs

Value of Graphs

Accountants use graphs to aid in transmitting information. Although they normally use numbers in textual or tabular form to report what has occurred or will occur, they can present the information in other ways—such as with visual aids. Each form of presentation has its advantages and should be judged by its effectiveness in communicating the salient ideas. Texts can explain and interpret. Texts use words, and words have shades of meaning that give us detail and that, more important, expand the meaning of a situation by conveying subtleties. Tables, using numbers, can provide comparisions and supporting evidence. Numbers are more precise than words. They have a finite relationship with each other. The exactness of numbers makes them particulary useful for comparisons and for providing precise details. Graphs can communicate and demonstrate relationships by means of pictures. Pictures conjure up mental images of an event by presenting it in visual form, personalizing the event for the viewer.

What criteria determine whether or not a particular graph will be effective in communicating information, including accounting results? The generally agreed-upon criteria are reliability, understandability, and an ability to attract and hold attention.

Reliability is highly valued by accountants and has been defined as "the faithfulness with which it (information) represents what it purports to represent."[1] The reason reliability is so important is that an essential characteristic of an accounting report is its acceptance, and if a report is considered to be misleading or superfluous, it and future reports will be disregarded.

Understandability implies that the graph will mean something

---

[1] Financial Accounting Standards Board, *Statement of Financial Accounting Concepts No. 2* (FASB, May 1980), p. 26.

3

to the audience. If the presentation has little meaning to the audience, it has little value. Understandability is the difference between data and information. Data are facts. Information is facts that mean something and make a difference to whoever receives them. Graphic presentation enhances understanding in a number of ways. Many people find that the visual comparison and contrast of information permit relationships to be grasped more easily. Relationships that had been obscure become clear and provide new insights.

Understanding involves both senders and receivers of information. Accountants (senders), by having to prepare and clarify what they want to convey, are forced to determine precisely what essential ideas are to be presented. They also must keep their audience in mind. The additional preparation needed to make graphs should stimulate a better and more thought-provoking presentation of the material. The audience (receivers) of the graph, to the extent that it is visually oriented, will find the graph a better source of new ideas than the standard textual report.

The third objective is to *attract and hold attention.* Communication isn't communication unless the message or thought is conveyed to the other party and means the same thing to the sender and to the receiver. One effective way of creating interest is by visual appeal. You can improve your knowledge of visual appeal by learning from good examples. Looking at examples of graphs in magazines, booklets, and annual reports can lead to recognition of well-presented graphs. Attention is important because unless the data attract and hold the attention of the audience, thereby creating or expanding interest in the information, the desired thought will not be conveyed. Attention is also believed to improve the thought process and the ability to analyze, which will increase retention.

Another advantage of graphic presentation is that, in a number of ways, it saves time. For one thing, when masses of data can be visualized at a glance, their essential meaning can be grasped more quickly. For another, the graphic presentation of flows, sequences, and relationships of data and concepts takes less space than words, reducing the time it takes to "read" the data.

Businesses use graphs in several ways. They use them in reports, such as annual reports to stockholders or reports of actual versus planned performances to management. They use them to present information at briefings, meetings, and conferences. Graphs also are used for analysis, planning, and scheduling and are helpful in supporting management decisions in matters such as site location, market analysis, productivity analysis, product planning, and media planning.

In summary, presenting financial information in graphic form increases reliability and understanding, attracts attention, and saves time by promoting a fuller and more balanced view of the material than can be provided in text form. Graphs are valuable to the extent that the user of the data can more readily grasp and retain the accounting meaning of the data presented in visual form than with a textual explanation. Graphs or visual aids, to be successful, should make a fact more explicit, a point of view more emphatic, a situation more visual.

Forms of Graphs

Before you can decide on the right graph, you have to know something about the available alternatives. Therefore, a brief discussion of graphs is in order. Examples pertaining to the following discussion can be found in Exhibit 1. (See page 7.) The basic form of a graph is established by placing one or more series of figures on a "coordinate surface." The x-axis or the horizontal scale is used for the independent variable, such as time, and the numbers go from left to right. The y-axis or the vertical scale is used for the dependent variable, such as revenue, with numbers going from bottom to top. The terms independent and dependent are similar to cause and effect. For example, a sailboat is moving and a wind is blowing. One can assume that the wind (independent variable) is causing the sailboat (dependent variable) to move. The movement of the boat is "dependent" on the wind.

Normally graphs use only one fourth of the coordinate surface, the one for which both sets of values are positive. Each series of figures is placed on the surface by identifying a point—the location of the two related variables, such as revenue for the month—for each figure of the series. If you want to distinguish one point from another, you can use different symbols, such as a closed (solid) circle and an open circle. The individual "points" can be joined together in a "line" or curve. This connection between two points (line) has a meaning. It may show, for example, the change in revenue between two months. Again, if you want to distinguish one line from another, you can use differing symbols, such as a solid line and a dashed line.

Besides points and lines, three other elements are used in preparation of graphs. They are shape, color, and texture. A shape is any two-dimensional form. Color has two components. The first is hue—what most people call color—blue, red, yellow. The second is intensity, which blends the hue with varying quantities of black or white, creating richness or depth of color. Texture is the surface structure, which can be varied from one area of a graph to another. They are all used to distinguish, emphasize, and attract attention.

There are many forms of graphs, some more suitable for accounting than others. The main types or forms of graphs used by accountants are line, area or surface, column, bar, and pie. These will be discussed, then examples shown in Exhibits 2 through 6. Other types, such as organization charts, flowcharts, scatter diagrams, semilogarithmic graphs, and pictorial graphs, are important in themselves but are not particularly suitable—or at least not widely used—for the presentation of accounting data. Detailed descriptions of the various forms of graphs can be found in reference books such as the one by Schmid and Schmid.[2] A brief comment on the latter two types of graphs is appropriate since accountants do use them occasionally.

The semilogarithmic graph has a logarithmic scale on the vertical axis and an arithmetic scale on the horizontal axis. This graph is good for representing relative change, such as proportional or percentage relationships. It is unique in that a series increasing by a constant *rate* is represented by a straight line on a semilogarithmic graph, whereas a series increasing by a constant *amount* would be represented by a straight line on an arithmetic graph.

The pictorial graph uses pictures as symbols to represent comparisons, usually over time. This graph can be extremely effective. Although it provides little or no more information than other forms of graphs, it is dramatic and creates interest. If poorly done, however, it can be distracting and misleading rather than attractive and representative of the facts.

Frequently Used Graphs

We now turn our attention to line, area or surface, column, bar, and pie graphs, the graphs commonly used to present accounting information. The line graph, a set of points connected by a line, is the simplest and therefore probably the most widely used visual presentation. It uses a curve (line) to show change over time, such as months, quarters, or years. The graph is used primarily to show movement, trends, or variation in a variable over time. The second, and less frequent, use is to show relationships between two variables. Examples of line graphs can be found in Exhibit 2 (page 8).

---

[2]Calvin F. Schmid and Stanton E. Schmid, *Handbook of Graphic Presentation*, 2nd ed. (New York: Ronald Press, 1979), p. 308.

Exhibit 1
Producing a Graph

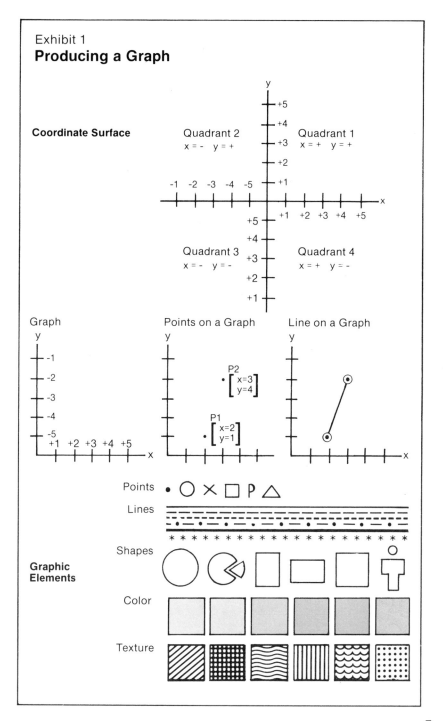

Coordinate Surface

Quadrant 2
x = - y = +

Quadrant 1
x = + y = +

Quadrant 3
x = - y = -

Quadrant 4
x = + y = -

Graph

Points on a Graph

Line on a Graph

P2 [x=3 y=4]

P1 [x=2 y=1]

Points

Lines

Shapes

Graphic Elements

Color

Texture

Exhibit 2
Line Graphs

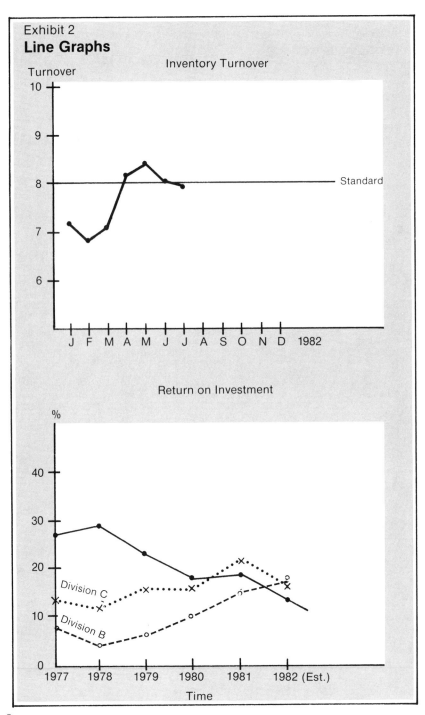

Inventory Turnover

Turnover

Standard

J F M A M J J A S O N D 1982

Return on Investment

%

Division C

Division B

1977 1978 1979 1980 1981 1982 (Est.)

Time

8

Exhibit 3
Area or Surface Graphs

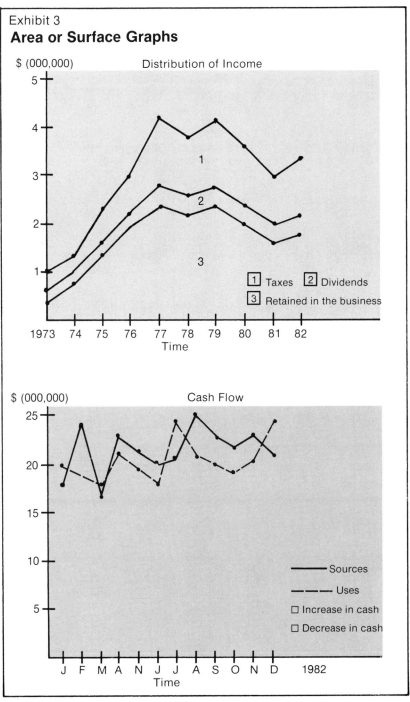

$ (000,000)   Distribution of Income

1 Taxes   2 Dividends
3 Retained in the business

1973 74 75 76 77 78 79 80 81 82
Time

$ (000,000)   Cash Flow

——— Sources
—–—– Uses
□ Increase in cash
□ Decrease in cash

J F M A N J J A S O N D   1982
Time

9

Exhibit 4
Column Graphs

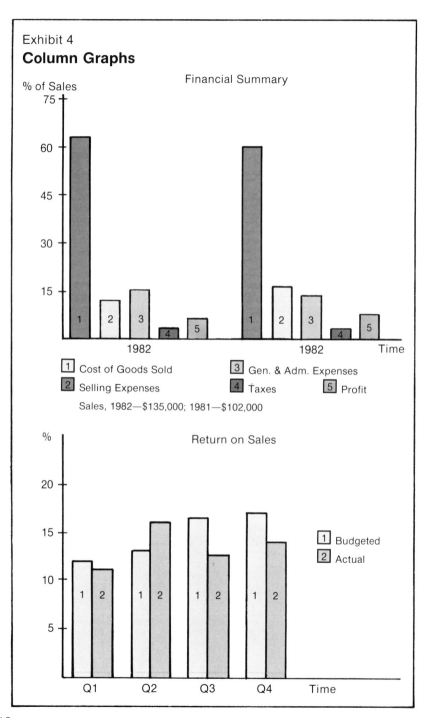

Financial Summary

% of Sales

1 Cost of Goods Sold   3 Gen. & Adm. Expenses
2 Selling Expenses   4 Taxes   5 Profit
Sales, 1982—$135,000; 1981—$102,000

Return on Sales

1 Budgeted
2 Actual

Exhibit 5
Bar Graphs

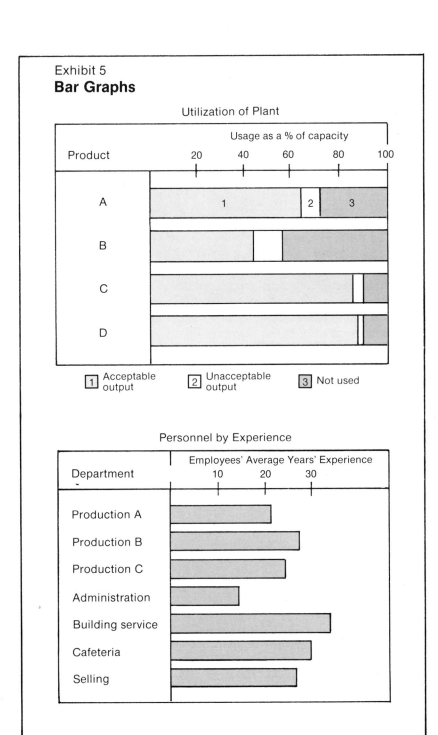

Utilization of Plant

Usage as a % of capacity

| Product | 20 | 40 | 60 | 80 | 100 |

A — 1 2 3

B

C

D

1 Acceptable output   2 Unacceptable output   3 Not used

Personnel by Experience

Employees' Average Years' Experience

| Department | 10 | 20 | 30 |

Production A

Production B

Production C

Administration

Building service

Cafeteria

Selling

There are several uses for which the line graph is particularly relevant. One is for a series of data covering a long period of time. Another is for comparing several series on the same graph. A third is for emphasizing the movement of data rather than the amount of the data. It also can be used with two scales on the vertical axis, one on the right and another on the left, allowing different series to use different scales, and it can be used to present trends and forecasts. Accounting data break down into two types: those for a *point in time*, such as cash as of December 31, 1983; and those for a *period* of time, such as revenue for December 1983. Either type of data can be "plotted" (recorded) on a line graph.

The area or surface graph is a variation of the line graph that can be used to present the same kinds of data in a more dramatic manner. This graph uses a shade pattern between each line to emphasize the variation among the lines. Examples can be found in Exhibit 3 (page 9). This graph is used to emphasize the data on a time series or trend line. A single trend line would use one of the various surface structures (texture) such as shading, cross-hatching, or even color to fill in the area between the trend and the base line. If there is more than one trend line on the graph, the shading will be varied to emphasize the differences between each line. The area or surface graph also can be used to accent some portion of the graph.

The column and bar graphs are similar in many ways; the main difference is that the column is vertical and the bar is horizontal. The same basic information can be presented in various graph forms. For example, when the points of a line chart are replaced with columns, one has a column graph. Examples of column graphs can be found in Exhibit 4 (page 10). Sometimes instead of the scale being in actual values, it can be in percentage values. These numerical values are indicated by the height of the columns.

Some Graphs Are More Versatile

The bar graph and the column graph are popular because they are simple and easy to read. These are the most versatile of the graph forms. They can be used to display time series, to display the relationship between two items, to make a comparison among several items, and to make a comparison between parts and the whole (total). They do not appear to be as "statistical," which is an advantage to those people who have negative attitudes toward statistics. The column graph shows values over time, and the bar graph shows values at a point in time. The bar graph compares different items as of a specific time (not over time). Examples of the bar graph can be found in Exhibit 5 (page 11). The bars originate at the left on the vertical or y-axis, which will list the items to be compared. The horizontal scale measures the value of each item, which is represented by the length of the bar.

The pie graph also is popular with accountants. This graph is divided into segments representing the distribution within each category. Examples can be found in Exhibit 6 (page 14). The pie graph is a circle whose area is divided into component parts. This type of graph makes a comparison of the segments and shows their relation to the whole. It is common to evaluate a section of the pie graph as the size of a "piece of pie." In reality, the significant measurement in a pie graph is the edge of that piece, or section of the circumference. Visually, the sections do not always appear to have the same size or value so, because of this perception, pie graphs can mislead.

These, then, are the major forms of graphs used by accountants—the line, area, and column graphs, which are used to show variables over time, and the bar and pie graphs, which are used to show variables as of a point in time. The line and area graphs are particularly suitable for showing change over time. The column graph also can be used for that purpose and for making comparisons over time. The bar graph can be used to compare items with one another at a point in time or to compare parts with the total. The pie graph is used to show component relationships as of a point in time.

Misrepresentation

Accountants have to be concerned that their reports do not mislead the users of the accounting statements. To avoid misleading, a report should mean the same to the preparer and the user. Technical wording and complicated accounting methodology can create a problem. The general, but not universally accepted, solution to this problem, according to some accountants, is for users to learn accounting rather than for accountants to prepare reports using nonaccounting terminology. The same set of problems holds true for the use of graphs to present accounting information. Is the level of sophistication of the users high enough so that communication can be assumed to exist (do the data have the same meaning to both parties)?

There are two kinds of misrepresentation. In one, the numerical data do not agree with the data in the graph, or certain relevant data are omitted. This kind of misleading presentation, while perhaps hard to determine, clearly is wrong and can be avoided. In the second kind of misrepresentation, the meaning of the data is differ-

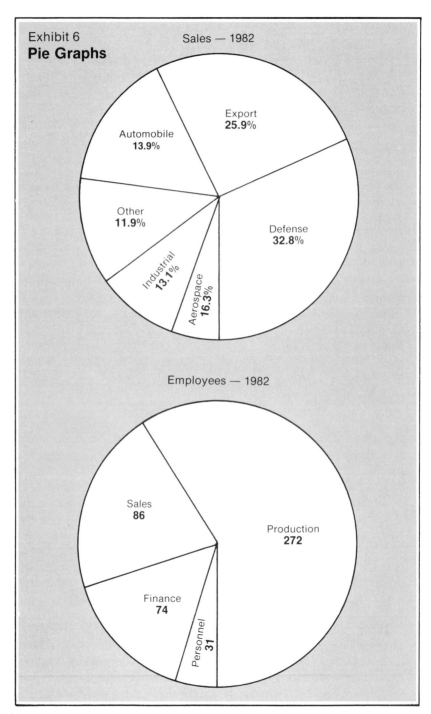

Exhibit 6
Pie Graphs

Sales — 1982

Export
25.9%

Automobile
13.9%

Other
11.9%

Defense
32.8%

Industrial
13.1%

Aerospace
16.3%

Employees — 1982

Sales
86

Production
272

Finance
74

Personnel
31

14

ent to the preparer and to the user. Who is to blame for this difference in connotation is not always clear. It can be caused by optical illusion if it looks like or appears to be something other than what it is. A simple example of two equal lines can show this.

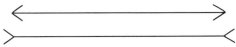

Picture graphs and pie graphs lend themselves to these kinds of illusion, or at least may make the data difficult to interpret.

Another reason for misunderstanding can be a differing extent of knowledge by the two parties. The level of audience sophistication that can be assumed varies from one as knowledgeable as the preparer's to one of little or no understanding about graphs. A recent journal article[3] presented the view that any assumption that the users of graphs have more than minimal knowledge of graphs is wrong, and therefore graphs using certain commonly accepted graphic techniques will mislead. Some typical graphic techniques that may cause problems are allowing for a break in the scale when there are no low numbers, using different scales for different trend lines, and using logarithmic scales to show rates of change. The authors of the article said the use of these kinds of techniques is, at best, confusing and, at worst, misleading to the typical user who does not understand the significance of graphic methodology.

There are other potential problems. Graphs are used to meet the need to condense all the available information into a more usable quantity. The selection process of combining and condensing will inevitably produce a less than complete study and will lead the user in certain directions, producing a potential for misleading.

Use of Color and Method of Display

The use of color provides clarity and impact; it highlights and associates. The color contrast is used to simplify complex data and display relationships. There has been little objective work to report the impact of color in graphs on the users. It generally is believed, however, that users are more inclined to be influenced by color graphs than by black-and-white graphs. It also is known that warm, bright colors tend to create positive impressions and dull, dark colors tend to create more negative impressions. This reaction

[3]Johnny R. Johnson, Richard R. Rice, and Roger A. Roemmich, "Pictures that Lie: The Abuse of Graphs in Annual Reports," *Management Accounting* (October 1980), pp. 50-56.

to color again provides a potential for misleading. For example, if you use two colors in a graph, a vivid blue and a dull gray, the blue will receive more attention and reduce the impact and significance of the gray symbol.

The way that graphs are displayed becomes important. On the one hand, the method of display must not inadvertently give false impressions. On the other hand, the display must ensure that the user sees everything pertinent to the data represented. The audience sophistication, the inclusion or exclusion of certain data, the selection of colors, the positioning of data—all have the potential for misleading the users of graphs.

Other aspects of graph preparation and presentation may be misleading. The scales used are important; contracting or expanding the vertical or horizontal scales will change the visual picture. The trend lines need enough grid lines to obviate difficulty in reading the results properly. One must be careful in the use of cross-hatching and shading, both of which can create illusions. Horizontal rulings tend to reduce the appearance, while vertical lines enlarge it. In summary, graphs must be reliable, and reliability depends not only on what is presented but also on how it is presented.

Graphic Designers

Once it has been decided to use a graphic presentation, some preliminary thought must be given to the form of the graph. A graph can be prepared in one of two ways. First, it can be hand drawn. The preparer may be an amateur (yourself) or a professional (graphic designer or artist). An example of a graph prepared by a graphic designer can be found in Exhibit 7.[4] (page 18) It is a pictorial graph. The exhibit uses the graph as part of a presentation to create an overall effect. The other way is to have it prepared by a computer, either your own or one from a computer service center.

An important part of preparation is deciding how the data are to be presented. Accountants usually have graphs reproduced for multiple-copy reports or use them as a supplementary aid for a verbal report. The reproduction would be by printing or a process of duplication. Graphs can be prepared in a hard copy to fit on a normal page—8½" by 11"—or in a larger poster size so they can be seen more easily or on 35mm slides so they can be shown on a screen. The appropriate selection depends on the intended use of the graphs.

---

[4]This graphic presentation was prepared by Butzko & Rosenthal Design Group, 214 Greenbrier Road, Fairfield, Conn. 06430.

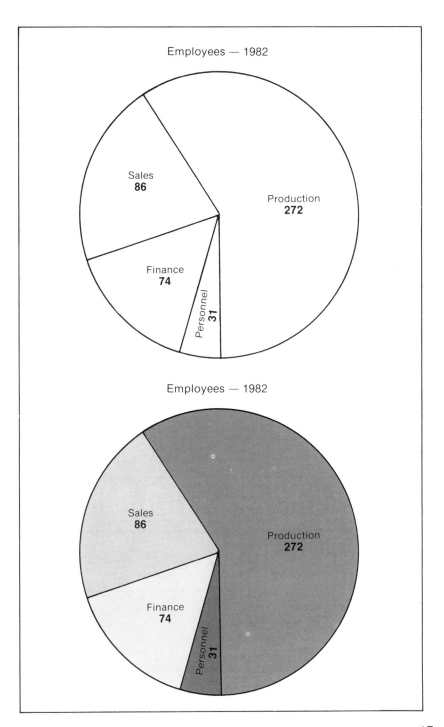

Employees — 1982

Sales
86

Production
272

Finance
74

Personnel
31

Employees — 1982

Sales
86

Production
272

Finance
74

Personnel
31

17

Exhibit 7

 Readership Study

Study

The Study	Focus on Clinical Laboratories 1981
Conducted by	Health Industries Research, Stamford, Connecticut David Labson, President
Who Surveyed	Directors of Clinical Laboratories, Chief Medical Technologists and Supervisors of Clinical Chemistry in Hospital and Independent Laboratories
Objective of Survey	Which of the 14 leading clinical journals best deliver these key audiences?
Journals Surveyed	American Journal of Clinical Pathology
	American Journal of Medical Technology
	Clinical Chemistry
	Clinical Chemistry News
	Clinical Lab Products
	Diagnostic Medicine
	Journal of the American Medical Technologists

Lab World*
Laboratory Management
Laboratory Medicine
Ligand Quarterly
Ligand Review
MLO/Medical Laboratory Observer
Pathologist

*Ceased publication

Results

Reading Frequency
Ranking of Laboratory Management
in Hospital and Independent Laboratories

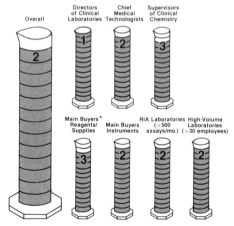

*Laboratory professionals responsible for buying
decisions or making the brand recommendations most
often followed

The main limitations on the use of graphs are time and cost. If you want a graph for a 10 a.m. meeting but it cannot be ready until 3, it is of little use. And people usually want to minimize the costs. The relative values of the two—time and cost—will vary with circumstances. Therefore, within your limitations, you have a graph prepared or even prepare your own graph. Often a neat, clear, simple graph is enough.

Assuming that you decide to use a graphic designer to make the graph, then what? What can you expect from a graphic designer? You expect the designer to be creative and to be able to produce an attractive individualized idea that works. Graphic designers' abilities vary, as do those of accountants. An accountant may be the single bookkeeper in a small firm or a chief financial officer in charge of several hundred people. A graphic designer is one who prepares or "lays out" any publication. A person who prepares a letter for publication is a graphic designer. A group that prepares an annual report for publication also consists of graphic designers.

However, there is an attempt to reserve the title of accountant or graphic designer for those who have had extensive training in their respective field, and the term *graphic designer* will be used in that reserved way. In the case of both the accountant and the graphic designer, one has to decide what degree of skill is needed. If the organizational needs are large, the graphic designers can be employees (perhaps specialized). If the organizational needs are small, the designer can be hired as a consultant to do a single job or a few jobs.

The more unusual or the less standardized the presentation desired, the more a skilled preparer of the material is needed. You need little skill to take a graph that was used last month and change the figures. If you want a "new" picture graph that has been adapted to the specific situation and want it to stand out, you need a graphic designer.

However, graphs are only one special area of expertise for a graphic designer. The designer should be able to help make the entire presentation attractive and effective. The designer can assist in choosing the kind of graph, the colors to be used, the size of type, the placement, the points to be emphasized, the use of empty space to avoid clutter, the kind of paper (including color and texture), the needs regarding mailing and/or handling, and many other points to make the entire presentation look its best.

A graphic designer knows production opportunities and limitations. She or he knows the various means of reproduction, especially printing, and should have a knowledge of photographs in addition to design layout. The layout of the graph and copy often is more important to the appearance and ability to create attention than the graph and copy themselves. The layout is putting the copy and graphics together and preparing the "boards" or "mechanicals" for the printer. Someone has to do it; therefore you need some kind of designer. It is only a question of how skilled that designer should be. The graphic designer has an edge because of his or her earlier mentioned qualities.

How do you choose a graphic designer? Let's assume that you are going to use the designer as a consultant rather than as an employee, although these comments are not unrelated to the selection of an employee. The most common way to choose a graphic designer is by recommendation. Another common way is by having seen examples of his or her work.

The designer, of course, has to be someone in the proper price range and geographic location. The cost of a graphic designer varies with the complexity of the graph. In 1983, in New York City, the cost of a standard graph is in the $50 to $100 range. Also, you usually would select a designer who specializes in your needs. You especially want someone with whom you can work. To summarize, the graphic designer must be able to meet your time and cost budget. He or she should be able to demonstrate experience with the kinds of graphs needed by showing samples of work done. There should be a personal interaction and communication between the two of you.

You As the Client

What is your role as the client? The main thing is to have a general basic idea of what you want and to communicate that idea to the graphic designer. You must supply enough information for the designer to be able to start work. For example, is the publication to be one page long or 16 pages? What size will it be? Do you want photographs or drawings? Where and when is the publication to be used? Who is the audience? Also, you should bring all the supplementary data, including photographs, artwork, and logo, to the graphic designer to help him or her understand what you want to accomplish. Finally the two of you must agree on the deadline and the budget for the project.

You should examine the first draft of the layout carefully to determine if you are satisfied and what changes need to be made. The earlier the changes can be made, the better. The material should be acceptable before the final copy is made so as not to waste time and money. Your most important role is to communicate correctly with the designer so that both of you agree on what is wanted. The designer should not have to guess what you want; his or her assumptions may be wrong. As was said earlier, a personal interaction and communication between the two of you is vital. Finally, you should be happy with the finished product; it is a combined effort of yours and the designer's and should be a unique and satisfying result.

Computer Graphics

The preparation of graphs by computers is becoming more popular as the costs of computer hardware decline and the necessary software becomes more available. The output of computer graphs is either in 35mm slides, permanent (hard) copy, or terminal displays (soft copy). The main advantage of a computer always has been its ability to handle large amounts of data very quickly. Traditionally, the computer has reported the data in written form. Computer graphics merely report the data in visual form. Graphs can be prepared faster by computers than by hand, which helps provide more timely reports. An example of a graph prepared by a computer can be found in Exhibit 8 (page 22).[5] The presentation uses pie graphs with color and texture to compare the source and use of funds during a period.

An economic justification for computer graphics is that the organization spends an enormous amount of money on data processing, often providing managers with too many reports, too many data, and an overload of information. The report output has to be condensed into a more usable form. The computer graph essentially is the data represented in a structured pictorial form. The role of the graph is to provide meaningful reports. To the extent that it does, it can be justified.

Management's main objections to the use of computer graphics are that they are too costly and that the quality of the graphs is not up to management's expectations. The latter is partly because a computer system does not automatically produce effective, useful graphs. The users have to know what to ask for, and many users are not familiar with good-quality computer graphics. (A simple and thorough coverage of this topic can be found in *Choosing the Right*

---

[5]This graph was prepared by Graphwriter from Graphic Communications, Inc., 200 Fifth Ave., Waltham, Mass., 02254.

Exhibit 8

SAINT-GOBAIN
sources and uses of funds
in millions of francs

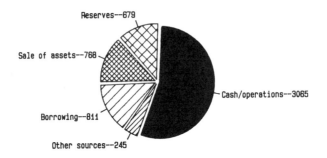

sources

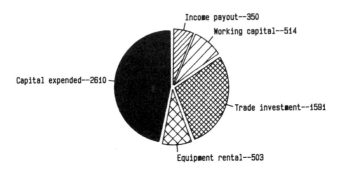

uses

Prepared by Graphwriter from
Graphic Communications, Inc.
200 Fifth Avenue, Waltham MA 02254

Chart.[6]) The selection of graphs should be based on inherent characteristics of the data and the users' objectives.

Users of graphs are not only accountants, but also engineers, planners, marketing analysts, and problem solvers of all kinds. As a result, the type of equipment required will be related to a great extent to all the users' needs, not just the accountants'.

Service Bureau

A firm that wants to have graphs prepared by a computer can take any of three approaches. The first is to use a service bureau. The firm would prepare a description of what it wants and send it to the bureau center, which would prepare a custom-made graph to the specifications. It would have graphic specialists who would help determine and prepare the data that are required and discuss the formats that might be suitable for the purpose.

There are no fixed costs, such as for hardware or software, on the part of the firm. The only cost is variable, the price per graph, which tends to be high. However, the service center can create high-quality graphs in minimum time. This approach is appropriate for a firm using few graphs or for a firm that wishes to try computer graphics without a large cash outlay. More information about service bureaus, their costs, and the other approaches to be discussed can be found in Appendix A.

Time-Sharing

The second approach to the preparation of computer graphs is time-sharing. This approach is subject to some fixed costs for rental of input equipment such as terminals and, if desired, output equipment such as printers, plotters, and camera devices. The variable cost per unit of graphs prepared is less, however, so whether the average cost per unit is less depends on volume. This approach is suitable for a reasonable number of graphs. Although the number would vary with the cost of the time-sharing, probably 50 to 75 a month would be needed. Time-sharing companies provide customer assistance, but the graphs are prepared by the firm's computer operators.

The simplest approach to time-sharing is to rent a remote terminal, which consists of a screen and keyboard connected to the service center's processing computer. One prepares a graph on the screen, using the typewriter-like keyboard. They keys will provide

---

[6]Alan Paller, Kathryn Szoka, and Nan Nelson, *Choosing the Right Chart* (Washington D.C.: ISSCO Graphics, 1981), pp. vii, 39.

the format, colors, lines, shapes, symbols, and text. The design can be changed as one works on it. When the graph is completed on the screen to the firm's satisfaction, it is transmitted via telephone to the processsing computer, which prepares the results in the desired form and ships the finished product to the firm. The results are either a 35mm slide or a hard-copy display, depending on your needs.

In-House Installation

Another approach is to put in an in-house installation. The firm would add computer graphic capability to its existing operation. It would have to lease or purchase the hardware and software necessary to produce computer graphs. They could be connected to the main company computer or be a separate "standalone" graphic computer. The firm also would need trained personnel. The initial outlay in money and time to become operational might be high, but this system would increase control over the firm's reports, provide maximum flexibility, and, with a large volume, produce the minimum per-unit cost. The appropriate approach depends, in good part, on the number of graphs the firm uses.

Whichever approach is used, a computer operator will prepare the graph on the computer. The operator could be you or your agent. In either case, you or your agent must select and specify the data to be "mapped." The selected data must be manipulated and organized to fit the available programs and equipment. An exploration has to be done and a decision on the alternative formats (available graph forms) has to be made. Then someone has to decide how to display the data on the graph to emphasize their significant features.

This completes the introduction to graphic presentation. You have learned the importance of graphs, what kinds there are, the importance of ensuring that the graphs are reliable, and how they can be prepared. Now it is time to look at how they currently are being used.

Chapter 2

Description of Current Practice

Kinds of Graphs

The current practice in reporting accounting information by graphs is interesting. Firms that use graphs as a part of managerial accounting reports were contacted through National Association of Accountants' chapters. Forty-one firms discussed their use of graphs, answering questions about how visual aids are used to present accounting information in their firms. Also, most of them provided samples of currently used graphs. To ensure confidentiality, the graphs will not be identified by firm.

The respondents varied in size, location, activities, and levels. In size the firms were from the top 20 to those that would not be included in the top 20,000. There were a significant number whose names are known nationally and also a significant number that are known only locally. They were located from Massachusetts to California, from Louisiana to Minnesota. More were from Pennsylvania (six) than from any other state. The firms include banks, hospitals, utility companies, manufacturers (both light and heavy), food processing firms, service firms, and others. The levels include corporate headquarters, groups, divisions, and local plants. It is a varied group of respondents.

The graphs submitted varied from simple hand-drawn graphs to elaborate and detailed graphic presentations. One firm submitted a package report that provided detailed monthly operating results of its firm. It consisted of 32 graphs (two to a page). They were in color and were combined column and line graphs. They displayed results of each month of last year and the average of the previous two years. The coverage of the graphs included receivables, inventories, revenues by categories, variances, and expenses.

When the respondents answered the questions, they described the kinds of graphs used, but the sample graphs they sent did not agree with those descriptions. They said one thing and showed another. Of course, it is possible that the graphs submitted did not reflect actual use. The middle column of Table 1 below illustrates the kinds of graphs used according to a questionnaire filled out by the firms. The column on the right shows the kinds of graphs being used according to the sample graphs submitted by the firms. In the middle column, since firms use more than one kind of graph, the total number will add up to more than the firms that answered. In the third column, each graph was classified as one category, so that number will add up to 142, the number submitted.

TABLE 1. Graphs Described by Firms versus Graphs Submitted

Type of Graph	Number of Firms Using Each Type	Number of Graphs Per Sample
Area or Surface	13	7
Bar	35	3
Column	23	18
Line	38	62
Pie	22	9
Other	19	—
Combinations	—	43

Although bar graphs were named as one category of the more popularly used graphs, the sample does not bear this out. There is a possiblity of confusion in names, and perhaps column graphs are being called bar graphs. In any case, the most commonly used graph form was the line graph, and the most common graphic report is on operational performance, updated monthly.

For example, Exhibit 9 (pages 28 and 29) depicts a graphic report on the operating performance of a bank using a number of line graphs. With this graphic report, one can in capsule form review the overall performance of a bank. The report provides the current actual results of a number of key indicators—interest margin, deposits, loans, and investments. Two "standards" also are provided—last year's actual and the current budget. The evaluation of performance requires a comparison of a measure of performance with a standard of adequacy of performance.

Another graphic report, Exhibit 10 (page 30), includes part of a manufacturing performance report. This is for a manufacturing plant that reports to a division that reports to a group that reports to corporate headquarters. The format is uniform among all plants.

The top graph shows the amount of scrap (wastage) caused directly by the manufacturing process. The bottom graph shows the number of tools and abrasives used directly on the product. These are examples of reports providing the results of a small aspect of operations. Graphs can be used to provide information about overall results or about narrow, specialized results.

One of the interesting findings from the sample of graphs was that a significant number of them are a combination of two forms of graphs. A representative combination graph is shown in Exhibit 11 (pages 32 and 33). A firm uses it in its monthly financial and operating report to management and the board of directors. Again, it is an overall indicator. Two of the major measures of performance are revenue and income. Standards or expectations in the form of budgets are provided so that not only results but also an indication of the quality of the results is available. Additional kinds of graphs will be shown in the section on their uses. There were 19 "other" types of graphs reported by the firms. Nine were semilogarithmic, six were pictorial, and one each fell into the category of miscellaneous graphs.

Displaying Graphs

Graphs can be displayed in a number of ways. Sometimes a temporary graph for personal use is all that is needed. If you have computer graphics you can show a graph on a TV-like screen called a cathode-ray tube (CRT) terminal. Because this form of display is not transportable and requires computer capability, it has only limited uses. Graphs from a CRT terminal cannot be shown in a report or publication, so you usually need a permanent form. Permanent graphs often are called hard copies. The forms of hard copies of graphs are transparencies, which are used with an overhead projector; 35mm slides, which are used in slide presentations; and paper reproductions, which are included in written reports or used as displays.

The most commonly prepared form, according to our correspondents, is the letter size or smaller hard copy, as either a transparency or a paper reproduction. All but two of the 41 firms used this form of graph. Nineteen of them used only hand-drawn ones, nine used only computer-drawn ones, and 11 used both.

Another common type was larger than letter size, such as the flip charts used by 20 companies. Fourteen of them used solely hand-drawn ones, two used solely computer-drawn ones, and four used both means of preparation. The third common form was 35mm slides, used by 23 firms. Fourteen used hand-drawn, and 11 used

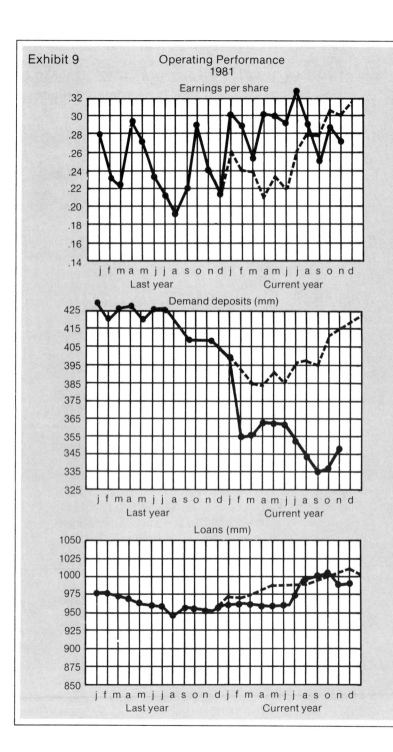

Exhibit 9

Operating Performance
1981

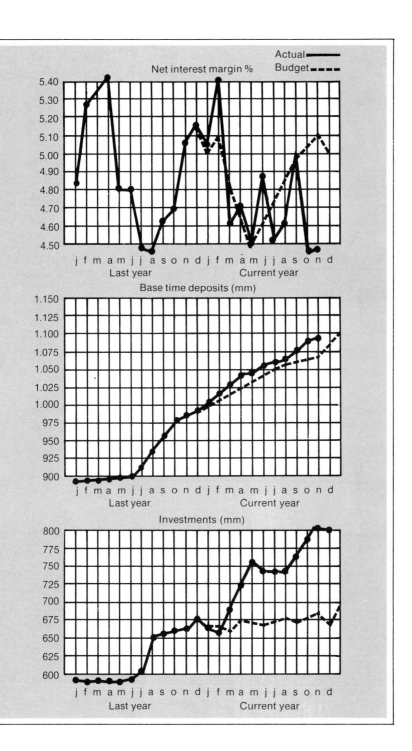

Exhibit 10

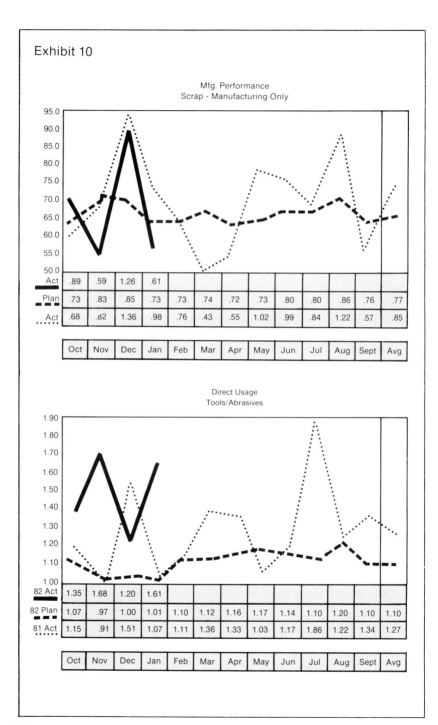

Mfg. Performance
Scrap - Manufacturing Only

	Oct	Nov	Dec	Jan	Feb	Mar	Apr	May	Jun	Jul	Aug	Sept	Avg
Act	.89	.59	1.26	.61									
Plan	.73	.83	.85	.73	.73	.74	.72	.73	.80	.80	.86	.76	.77
Act	.68	.82	1.36	.98	.76	.43	.55	1.02	.99	.84	1.22	.57	.85

Direct Usage
Tools/Abrasives

	Oct	Nov	Dec	Jan	Feb	Mar	Apr	May	Jun	Jul	Aug	Sept	Avg
82 Act	1.35	1.68	1.20	1.61									
82 Plan	1.07	.97	1.00	1.01	1.10	1.12	1.16	1.17	1.14	1.10	1.20	1.10	1.10
81 Act	1.15	.91	1.51	1.07	1.11	1.36	1.33	1.03	1.17	1.86	1.22	1.34	1.27

30

computer-drawn slides. Two firms included in the above count used both methods to prepare slides.

Graphs can be prepared by the accounting department, by a separate unit, or jointly by the two units. About half the firms had some graphs made by the accounting department and some by a separate unit. Counting only these firms, the average percentage of the graphs prepared by the accounting department was 60%. The rest were prepared by the separate unit. Ten firms prepared all the graphs in the accounting department, seven had all the graphs prepared solely by a separate unit, and only three of the firms prepared all their graphs jointly.

Turnaround Time

One of the more important considerations when dealing with graphs is the turnaround time between request and receipt. It is less significant for the routinely prepared reports, although it slows the preparation and reduces the timeliness of the reports. But for the special reports, especially the unexpected ones, turnaround time may prevent the use of graphs. The range of time needed varied from a few minutes to four weeks; the median time was three days. However, 13 of the 41 firms had a turnaround time of 24 hours or less.

If the time necessary to prepare the graphs is longer than the available time, you might examine the procedures for expediting preparation. Fewer than half the firms had procedures for doing this. The most common procedure was to request that the graphs be prepared faster, often for an additional charge. The second most common means was improved scheduling by planning ahead, which is not always possible. Several indicated that applying pressure helped, with one respondent reporting his method of getting a graph quickly: "Persistent badgering and veiled threats work best."

Use of Graphs

Graphs are used for two different types of activities—analysis and presentation. Analysis is one of the tools used in decision making. For example, in an alternative choice decision, one would forecast the results under each of the alternatives and select the one that most advances the objectives. Graphs can be used to display the differing forecasted results to enable the user to understand them better. Graphs for this purpose can be terminal displays or hard copy. The quality has only to be good enough not to distract. Neatness and accuracy are all that are needed.

Exhibit 11

Consolidated Revenue

| | $ thousands | | | % increase | |
	1981	Budget	1980	1981	1980
January	229,386	211,868	170,496	35	26
February	201,744	195,923	156,459	29	31
March	235,665	209,526	210,780	13	80
April	208,132	176,790	140,129	49	27
May	208,872	170,697	130,220	60	24
June	194,969	170,168	114,460	70	14
July	197,710	168,330	121,659	63	15
August	202,266	172,366	121,779	66	9
September	182,921	166,860	119,165	54	—
October	217,034	187,896	138,407	57	3
November	232,995	207,704	153,000	52	11
December	258,949	233,512	168,427	54	15
Year	2,570,643	2,271,640	1,744,981	47	21

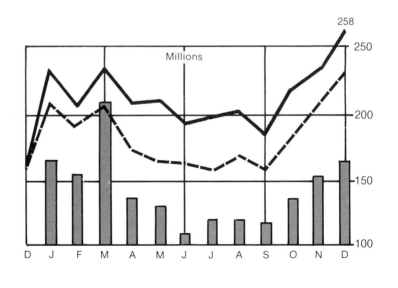

Consolidated Net Income

	$ thousands			% increase	
	1981	Budget	1980	1981	1980
January	16,036	15,740	14,142	13	—
February	16,256	14,114	11,355	43	52
March	15,056	14,130	11,553	30	32
April	11,594	14,708	8,005	45	(18)
May	13,926	15,596	11,198	24	19
June	12,476	14,534	11,545	8	46
July	6,628	14,381	9,850	(33)	21
August	13,844	13,745	11,614	19	27
September	16,158	12,171	14,840	9	69
October	15,168	10,209	7,889	92	(27)
November	10,503	14,864	14,256	(26)	98
December (1)	26,027	16,553	20,910	24	26
Year (1)	173,672	170,745	147,157	18	25

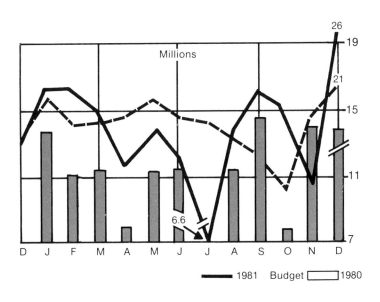

Presentation is one party reporting on a topic to another party. Graphs are used to present supporting data and to aid in the comprehension and retention of the points made. The audience for the graphs is important. Graphs used in presentations should be of a higher quality and be better looking because the appearance of the graph may help convince or even impress an audience. To summarize, graphs used for analysis need convey the information just to oneself, while graphs used for presentaton need to communicate information to others. Although not expressly stated, we assume that the graphs submitted by the respondents were presentation graphs.

The graphs were prepared for many different users. The major one was top management, with 38 of the 41 respondents preparing graphs for this group. Other major users were middle management (35) and department meetings (27).

The major classifications of accounts in accounting are revenue, expenses, assets, liabilities, and equity. Graphs could be used to present information about any of these accounts, although in reality the reporting of accounting information by graphs is heavy in the first three groups and very light in the latter two. Thirty-one of the firms that use graphs reported using them for all three—revenue, expenses, and assets—and an additional eight reported using them for two of the three. Few graphs are used to report on liabilities and equities, and they are usually on income or earnings per share.

The graphs submitted by our respondents usually reported on one of the accounts. First, look at the revenue account. Graphs showing some aspect of revenue were quite common. They often were used to make comparisons. Although line graphs were used most often, the other graph forms were not neglected. The column graph, for example, is a good graph for making comparisons, such as comparing the sales of a firm with those of its major competitor. See Exhibit 12. Pie graphs can be used to compare a part to the whole, as is done in the graph at the bottom of Exhibit 12. This graph shows the geographic distribution of a firm's sales.

Some graphs provide more detail about the revenue than just total amount. For example, in firms that produce for order rather than for inventory, the number of orders and amount of backlog are extremely important. The longer the manufacturing time, the more important backlog becomes. A line graph can be used to provide information about orders and backlogs, in both absolute and comparative terms, as in Exhibit 13 (page 36).

Another classification of accounts is expenses. A plurality of the

34

Exhibit 12

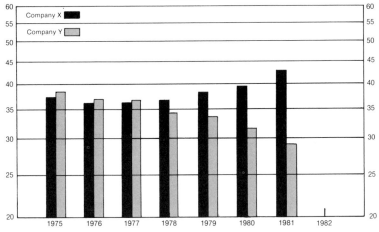

Sales Comparison
terms: millions

Company X
Company Y

1975 1976 1977 1978 1979 1980 1981 1982

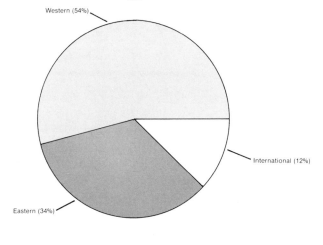

Marketing Area Percent of Sales
1981

Western (54%)

International (12%)

Eastern (34%)

Exhibit 13

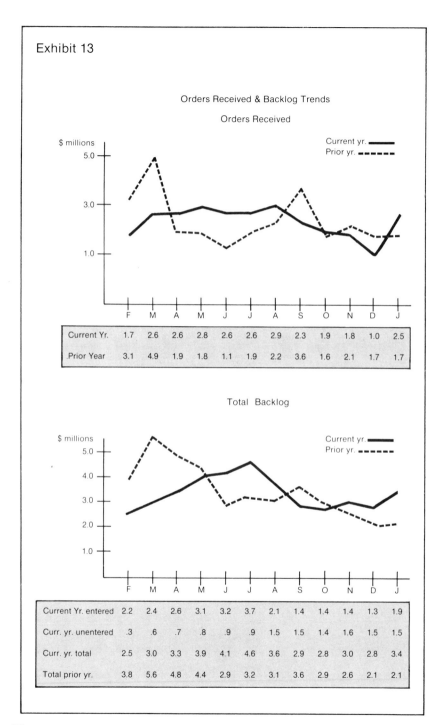

Orders Received & Backlog Trends

Orders Received

	F	M	A	M	J	J	A	S	O	N	D	J
Current Yr.	1.7	2.6	2.6	2.8	2.6	2.6	2.9	2.3	1.9	1.8	1.0	2.5
.Prior Year	3.1	4.9	1.9	1.8	1.1	1.9	2.2	3.6	1.6	2.1	1.7	1.7

Total Backlog

	F	M	A	M	J	J	A	S	O	N	D	J
Current Yr. entered	2.2	2.4	2.6	3.1	3.2	3.7	2.1	1.4	1.4	1.4	1.3	1.9
Curr. yr. unentered	.3	.6	.7	.8	.9	.9	1.5	1.5	1.4	1.6	1.5	1.5
Curr. yr. total	2.5	3.0	3.3	3.9	4.1	4.6	3.6	2.9	2.8	3.0	2.8	3.4
Total prior yr.	3.8	5.6	4.8	4.4	2.9	3.2	3.1	3.6	2.9	2.6	2.1	2.1

Exhibit 14

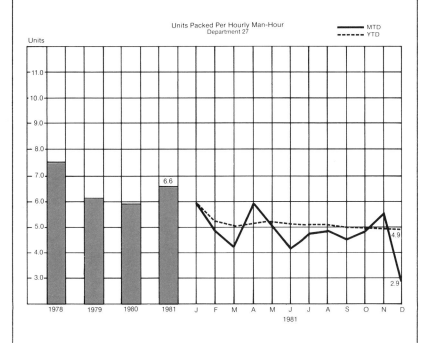

Units Packed Per Hourly Man-Hour
Department 27

Units

MTD
YTD

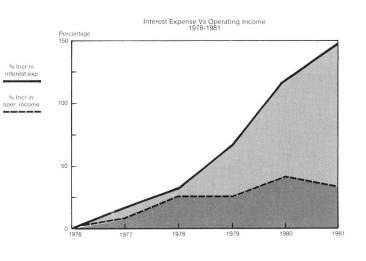

Interest Expense Vs Operating Income
1978-1981

Percentage

% Incr in
interest exp

% Incr in
oper. income

sample of graphs portrayed some aspect of expenses and/or costs. Some of these graphs have already been discussed. Then there is the production report in the form of a combined column and line graph. This is an example of a pictorial presentation of output per man-hour in a manufacturing plant. See Exhibit 14 (page 37). The lower graph in this exhibit—a line graph—is a forecast of the effect of interest on a highly leveraged firm. This firm is very concerned about interest costs since the availability and cost of borrowing will be prime determinants of its future growth.

The third major classification of accounts subject to graphic coverage is assets. Cash is a good place to start. There are several versions of cash flow graphs: pie graphs, line graphs, and the one shown in Exhibit 15, a column graph. This graph shows the cash (in) flow and cash outlay. Noticeable is the simplified but effective division of the two columns. At a glance one can see the change in cash during each part of that period.

Another frequent example was inventories. A series of line graphs in Exhibit 16 provides the total inventory and the major categories of inventory, comparing actual amounts with budgeted amounts and providing an indication of efficiency of use.

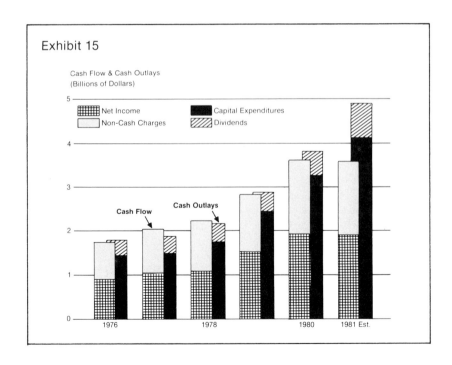

Exhibit 15

Cash Flow & Cash Outlays
(Billions of Dollars)

Net Income
Non-Cash Charges
Capital Expenditures
Dividends

Cash Flow
Cash Outlays

1976   1978   1980   1981 Est.

Exhibit 16

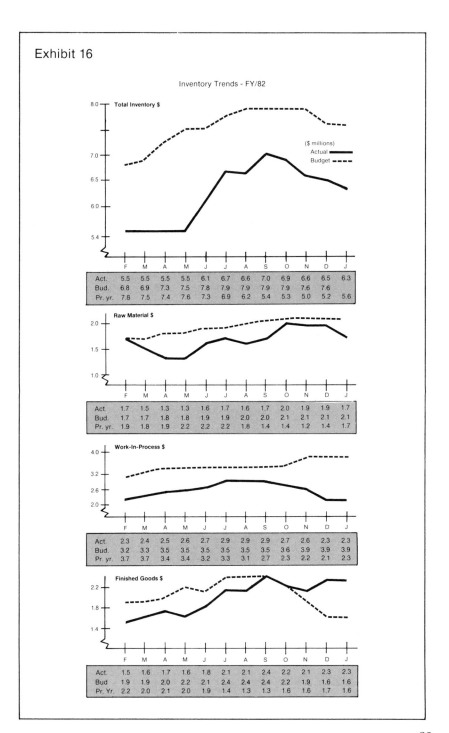

Inventory Trends - FY/82

Total Inventory $

($ millions)
Actual ▬▬
Budget ▬ ▬ ▬

	F	M	A	M	J	J	A	S	O	N	D	J
Act.	5.5	5.5	5.5	5.5	6.1	6.7	6.6	7.0	6.9	6.6	6.5	6.3
Bud.	6.8	6.9	7.3	7.5	7.8	7.9	7.9	7.9	7.9	7.6	7.6	
Pr. yr.	7.8	7.5	7.4	7.6	7.3	6.9	6.2	5.4	5.3	5.0	5.2	5.6

Raw Material $

	F	M	A	M	J	J	A	S	O	N	D	J
Act.	1.7	1.5	1.3	1.3	1.6	1.7	1.6	1.7	2.0	1.9	1.9	1.7
Bud.	1.7	1.7	1.8	1.8	1.9	1.9	2.0	2.0	2.1	2.1	2.1	2.1
Pr. yr.	1.9	1.8	1.9	2.2	2.2	2.2	1.8	1.4	1.4	1.2	1.4	1.7

Work-In-Process $

	F	M	A	M	J	J	A	S	O	N	D	J
Act.	2.3	2.4	2.5	2.6	2.7	2.9	2.9	2.9	2.7	2.6	2.3	2.3
Bud.	3.2	3.3	3.5	3.5	3.5	3.5	3.5	3.5	3.6	3.9	3.9	3.9
Pr. yr.	3.7	3.7	3.4	3.4	3.2	3.3	3.1	2.7	2.3	2.2	2.1	2.3

Finished Goods $

	F	M	A	M	J	J	A	S	O	N	D	J
Act.	1.5	1.6	1.7	1.6	1.8	2.1	2.1	2.4	2.2	2.1	2.3	2.3
Bud	1.9	1.9	2.0	2.2	2.1	2.4	2.4	2.4	2.2	1.9	1.6	1.6
Pr. Yr.	2.2	2.0	2.1	2.0	1.9	1.4	1.3	1.3	1.6	1.6	1.7	1.6

39

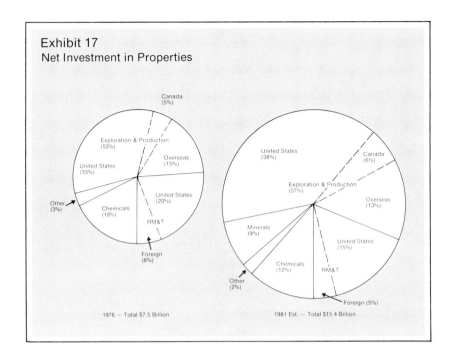

Exhibit 17
Net Investment in Properties

1976 — Total $7.5 Billion

1981 Est. — Total $15.4 Billion

The last example in this group is a pair of pie graphs comparing 1976 with 1981 for net investments in properties. These graphs (Exhibit 17) provide information about the geographic and functional investments at two points in time. Comparing the two makes the change in direction during the five-year period more evident.

Some constructive comments about the graphs used by the firms follow. The graphs, of course, varied tremendously, and the comments should not be considered descriptive of all graphs. The graphs mostly were in black and white; a greater use of color would improve attractiveness and attention-getting ability. Many graphs are prepared on heavy graph paper; the graph lines tend to distract from the presentation. The texture or shade patterns used to distinguish a column or an area in a graph is often too elaborate, if not garish. A simpler shading pattern going from darkest to lightest would improve the appearance. Frequently the labeling is inadequate, so that unless one is familiar with the coverage one cannot understand the presentation.

On a more positive note, the correspondents were generally happy with their graphs. The strengths, according to them, were clarity, simplicity, understandability, and improved communication and comprehension. The weaknesses, again according to them, were oversimplification and sometimes a too cluttered graph. The most common form of graph was the line graph, and the most common graphic report was one on operational performance that is updated monthly. The major uses of graphs were to present results and/or comparisons of various accounting catagories, such as revenue or cash. A final note: Graphs can be an effective supplementary method of presenting accounting information, especially to nonaccountants.

Summary

Management accountants must communicate and interpret data to the users. Graphs are one means of accomplishing these tasks. They can be used to show results, indicate trends, and make comparisons.

The accountant must select the right graphic presentation to maximize its communicative value. The graph must be reliable, be understandable, and attract attention. If you want to use graphs, you must be familiar with the major forms in which they appear—line, bar, column, area, and pie. You should know, for example, which are suitable for time series data (line, area, and column graphs). Bar and pie graphs are better at showing results at a point in time.

Because reliability is important to the accountant, the graphs must be prepared to minimize misrepresentation. One needs to remember that the perception of the user is not necessarily that of the preparer. In addition, you should be familiar with what graphic designers can do and what computer graphics can do so that either or both can be used properly.

A major part of this report is the description of current practice in reporting accounting information by graphs. Forty-one firms of varying size, location, and activities answered questions about their use of graphs and sent 142 different sample graphs. The graphs varied from simple, hand-drawn ones to elaborate and detailed graphic presentations.

Appendix A

State of the Art in Computer Graphics

The state of the art in computer graphics is changing so rapidly that this review may be out of date before it is published. However, it is written to give an idea of what computer graphics were like in early 1982. Although the names and dollar costs will change, the 1982 data should represent a starting point.

Sales of computer graphics equipment in 1980 (latest available figures) were $1.3 billion, and business graphs accounted for 28% of this amount. Both the total and the proportion devoted to business are expected to increase significantly in the next few years.

Historically, the interest in business computer graphs has been to produce the same type of graphs currently in use, but faster and at lower cost. One approach to having graphs prepared by a computer is to use a service bureau. There are a number of them. The data are brought to the service center, where the graphs are prepared on a computer and delivered to the client. One of the service bureaus is Xerox, which has 48 centers throughout the United States. The centers will prepare slides, transparencies, or hard-copy graphs on their computers. The minimum charge is $25, $5, and $2.90, respectively. The actual cost of the slide or transparency depends on the complexity of the graph. The cost of hard copies depends on the quantity.

Another service bureau is Genigraphics, a division of General Electric. This service bureau specializes in slides. The minimum cost is $15 per slide, with the actual cost depending on the number of plot points and the specialized background. The company has a large number of special effects that can be placed on the slides and 40 different formats for graphs. The graphs are prepared by artists on a computer, a black-and-white hard copy is given to the client for editing, and the slide is delivered in five working days. If the slide is needed sooner, it can be provided at an additional cost. This firm has 17 centers in the United States.

You can buy a computer that specializes in making graphs. It had been believed that economies of scale would centralize data processing. However, small computers have become so inexpensive that an organization can buy several small computers to do the work as cheaply as one large central computer and allow more individual department control as well. The inexpensive personal office computer has made it economical to automate activities previously preformed manually.

One specialized service that can be automated is the making of business graphs. Currently, for $3,145 or $4,245, you can buy a personal office computer (microcomputer) that will prepare elementary black-and-white or color graphs, respectively (Apple 3, $1,395; Disc drive, $650; Visiplot software package, $200; printer, black and white, $900; color, $2,000). These are basic graphic computers. If you wanted to produce any special graph, you would need better software and/or output units.

Software is so critical to the personal office computer buyers that experts say its cost will eventually exceed that of the hardware. Some firms preparing extensive software are already taking the position that one should select the software and then choose hardware that is compatible, rather than the other way around. One of these is Graphwriter. Although this firm sells a fully set up system, basically it sells software. It uses Hewlett-Packard equipment that is sold at retail for $10,000 and software that sells for $8,000. These costs can vary, depending on the quantity of output needed.

This system will prepare hard copy, transparencies, and slides. The slides are of moderate quality but very inexpensive; the only cost is that of processing the film, which can be done at any film processor. Genigraphics claims its system is easier to operate and requires a less skilled operator, thereby reducing operating costs. The training needed, according to Genigraphics, is less than two hours.

The graphics system can be a self-contained, standalone system as has been described, or it can consist of a device connected to a general-purpose host or main computer. If you wanted to use an existing computer, what would you need? According to IBM, you would need a terminal such as a 3297 color CRT, which costs $700, and software that would cost between $600 and $9,000, depending on complexity. Standard printers or plotters can be used for the output, but often firms do not have output units that reproduce in color.

Making computer graphs is just one more use of the data processing system. Whether to use a standalone system or one connected to the main computer should be decided on the basis of whether your organization has and wants a centralized or decentralized data processing system. There is no reason to treat graphs as anything different from other means of processing data.

A couple of points to remember: The limiting factor in computer graphics is memory. It takes a lot of memory to display a graph because each point on a graph, whether on a cathrode-ray tube (CRT) display or on hard copy, must be stored as one bit. The more bits (memory), the better the picture. The more bits, the higher the cost.

The second point to keep in mind is the concept called "user friendly," which means easy to use, requiring little, if any, training. This subjective concept refers to the degree of knowledge of computer terminology needed to use the equipment. The concept has to do with whether one needs programmer help. If a manager or other user is going to produce a graph directly, that person must be able to communicate with the computer. The two of them must speak the same language. The term "user friendly" is widely abused. Check out any software system to determine if the instructions are, in fact, easy to follow.

Appendix B

Contributors

Name	NAA Chapter
Donald M. Barkofsky	Bakersfield Area
D. A. Baumgartner,	
D. Bowalick, and V. Grant	Lancaster
Hamilton O. Beardsley	Northern Virginia
Wayne R. Bradshaw	South Jersey
Richard J. Brunner	Salt Lake Area
R. John Byrnes	Battle Creek
Roche J. Charanyhat	Cleveland
Diane C. Chiponis	Delaware County Pennsylvania
H. Allan Collins	Binghamton
Robert R. Davenport	Morristown
Warren F. Dedrick	Cleveland East
F. W. Desseau, Jr.	Mt. Rainier
George Dotzel	York
Michael B. Dowd	North Central Indiana
P. J. Duffy, Jr.	Toledo
Stephen M. Evans	Wabash Valley
D. Gendreau and D. Vigor	Providence
Al Goll	New York
Charles G. Hart	Central Arkansas
Paul Haun	Raleigh
Patricia J. Hykes	Harrisburg Area
R. N. Jameson, Jr.	East Tennessee
Michael Johnson	St. Paul
Jerry L. Kelley	Illowa

Becky A. Kilbourne	Albuquerque
Ira D. Levine	Birmingham-Magic City
Deborah A. Milowicki	Delaware
Bradford K. Mortz	Oakland
Ina G. Navarre	Baton Rouge
Herbert Plep	Portland Columbia
Brad D. Platts	Evansville
Michael Primini	Waterbury
James R. Rowe	Richmond Lee
Fred J. Saathoff	Chicago
Thomas J. Sandeman	Dayton
James F. Sanko	Beaver Valley
Surendra S. Singhvi	Miami Valley
Lorne D. Walker	Boston
Peter W. Walker	Dallas
Frank W. Wentz	Washington Tri-Cities
James L. Zamboldi	Altoona Area

National Association of Accountants Committee on Research 1982-1983

Notes

Notes

Notes

Notes